Hot Math Topics

Problem Solving, Communication, and Reasoning

Reasoning and Patterns

grade 2

Carole Greenes
Linda Schulman Dacey
Rika Spungin

Dale Seymour Publications®
Parsippany, New Jersey

Dale Seymour Publications
An imprint of Pearson Learning
299 Jefferson Road
Parsippany, New Jersey 07054-0480
800-321-3106
www.pearsonlearning.com

Editorial Manager: Carolyn Coyle
Project Editor: Mali Apple
Production/Manufacturing Director: Janet Yearian
Production/Manufacturing Manager: Karen Edmonds
Senior Production/Manufacturing Coordinator: Roxanne Knoll
Art Director: Jim O'Shea
Text Design: Tracey Munz
Cover Design: Elaine Lopez
Cover and Interior Illustrations: Jared Lee
Computer Graphics: Alan Noyes

ISBN 0-7690-0833-X

3 4 5 6 7 8 9 10-ML-04 03 02 01 00

This Book Is Printed
On Recycled Paper

Contents

Introduction

Why Was *Hot Math Topics* Developed?

The *Hot Math Topics* series was developed for several reasons:

- to offer children practice and maintenance of previously learned skills and concepts
- to enhance problem solving and mathematical reasoning abilities
- to build literacy skills
- to nurture collaborative learning behaviors

Practicing and maintaining concepts and skills

Although textbooks and core curriculum materials treat the topics explored in this series, their treatment is often limited by lesson format and page size. Consequently, there are often not enough opportunities for children to practice newly acquired concepts and skills related to the topics, or to connect the topics to other content areas. *Hot Math Topics* provides the necessary practice and mathematical connections.

Similarly, core instructional programs often do not do a very good job of helping children maintain their skills. Although textbooks do include reviews of previously learned material, they are often limited to sidebars or boxed-off areas on one or two pages in each chapter, with four or five exercises in each box. Each set of problems is intended only as a sampling of previously taught topics, rather than as a complete review. In the selection and placement of the review exercises, little or no attention is given to levels of complexity of the problems. By contrast, *Hot Math Topics* targets specific topics and gives children more experience with concepts and skills related to them. The problems are sequenced by difficulty, allowing children to hone their skills. And, because they are not tied to specific lessons, the problems can be used at any time.

Enhancing problem solving and mathematical reasoning abilities

Hot Math Topics present children with situations in which they may use a variety of problem solving strategies, including

- designing and conducting experiments to generate or collect data
- guessing, checking, and revising
- organizing data in lists or tables in order to identify patterns and relationships
- choosing appropriate computational algorithms and deciding on a sequence of computations
- using inverse operations in "work backward" solution paths

For their solutions, children are also required to bring to bear various methods of reasoning, including

- deductive reasoning
- inductive reasoning
- proportional reasoning

For example, to solve clue-type problems, children must reason deductively and make inferences about mathematical relationships in order to generate candidates for the solutions and to hone in on those that meet all of the problem's conditions.

To identify and continue a pattern and then write a rule for finding the next term in that pattern, children must reason inductively.

To find equivalent quantities and to make trades, children must reason proportionally.

To estimate or compare magnitudes of numbers, or to determine the type of number appropriate for a given situation, children must apply their number sense skills.

Building communication and literacy skills

Hot Math Topics offers children opportunities to write and talk about mathematical ideas. For many problems, children must describe their solution paths, justify their solutions, give their opinions, or write or tell stories.

Some problems have multiple solution methods. With these problems, children may have to compare their methods with those of their peers and talk about how their approaches are alike and different.

Other problems have multiple solutions, requiring children to confer to be sure they have found all possible answers.

Nurturing collaborative learning behaviors

Several of the problems can be solved by children working together. Some are designed specifically as partner problems. By working collaboratively, children can develop expertise in posing questions that call for clarification or verification, brainstorming solution strategies, and following another person's line of reasoning.

What Is in *Reasoning and Patterns*?

This book contains 100 problems and tasks that focus on finding patterns and using logical reasoning. The mathematics content, the mathematical connections, the problem solving strategies, and the communication skills that are emphasized are described below.

Mathematics content

Patterns and reasoning problems and tasks require children to

- complete, extend, create, and generalize repeating and growing patterns
- identify and apply function rules
- identify and describe similarities and differences among elements of a set and between sets
- use deductive, inductive, proportional, spatial, and algebraic reasoning to solve problems
- solve problems with variables
- apply numeration, number sense, and computation skills

Mathematical connections

In these problems and tasks, connections are made to these other topic areas:

- arithmetic
- algebra
- graphs
- measurement
- number theory

Problem solving strategies

Reasoning and Patterns problems and tasks offer children opportunities to use one or more of several problem solving strategies.

- **Formulate Questions:** When data are presented in displays or text form, children must pose one or more questions that can be answered using the given data.

- **Complete Stories:** When confronted with an incomplete story, children must supply the missing information and then check that the story makes sense.
- **Organize Information:** To ensure that several solution candidates for a problem are considered, children may have to organize information by drawing a picture, making a list, or completing a chart.
- **Guess, Check, and Revise:** In some problems, children have to identify or generate candidates for the solution and then check whether those candidates match the conditions of the problem. If the conditions are not satisfied, other possible solutions must be generated and verified.
- **Identify and Continue Patterns:** To identify the next term or terms in a sequence, children have to recognize the relationship between successive terms and then generalize that relationship.
- **Use Logic:** Children have to reason deductively, from clues, to make inferences about the solution to a problem. They have to reason inductively to continue patterns.
- **Work Backward:** In some problems, the output is given and children must determine the input by identifying mathematical relationships between the input and output and applying inverse operations.

Communication skills

Problems and tasks in *Reasoning and Patterns* are designed to stimulate communication. As part of the solution process, children may have to

- describe their thinking
- describe patterns
- find alternate solution methods and solution paths
- identify other possible answers
- formulate problems for classmates to solve
- compare solutions and methods with classmates
- make drawings to clarify mathematical relationships

These communication skills are enhanced when children interact with one another and with the teacher. By communicating both orally and in writing, children develop their understanding and use of the language of mathematics.

How Can *Hot Math Topics* Be Used?

The problems may be used as practice of newly learned concepts and skills, as maintenance of previously learned ideas, and as enrichment experiences for early finishers or more advanced students.

They may be used in class or assigned for homework. If used during class, they may be selected to complement lessons dealing with a specific topic or assigned every week as a means of keeping skills alive and well. Because the problems often require the application of various problem solving strategies and reasoning methods, they may also form the basis of whole-class lessons whose goals are to develop expertise with specific problem solving strategies or methods.

The problems, which are sequenced from least to most difficult, may be used by children working in pairs or on their own. The selection of problems may be made by the teacher or the children based on their needs or interests. If the plan is for children to choose problems, you may wish to copy individual problems onto card stock and laminate them, and establish a problem card file.

To facilitate record keeping, a Management Chart is provided on page 6. The chart can be duplicated so that there is one for each child. As a problem is completed, the space corresponding to that problem's number may be shaded. An Award Certificate is included on page 6 as well.

How Can Children's Performance Be Assessed?

Reasoning and Patterns problems and tasks provide you with opportunities to assess children's

- pattern recognition and generation abilities
- mathematical reasoning methods
- knowledge of number concepts, skills, and relationships among numbers
- problem solving abilities
- communication skills

Observations

Keeping anecdotal records helps you to remember important information you gain as you observe children at work. To make observations more manageable, limit each observation to a group of four to six children or to one of the areas noted above. You may find that using index cards facilitates the recording process.

Discussions

Many of the *Reasoning and Patterns* problems and tasks allow for multiple answers or may be solved in a variety of ways. This built-in richness motivates children to discuss their work with one another. Small groups or class discussions are appropriate. As children share their approaches to the problems, you will gain additional insights into their content knowledge, mathematical reasoning, and communication abilities.

Scoring responses

You may wish to holistically score children's responses to the problems and tasks. The simple scoring rubric below uses three levels: high, medium, and low.

Portfolios

Having children store their responses to the problems in *Hot Math Topics* portfolios allows them to see improvement in their work over time. You may want to have them choose examples of their best responses for inclusion in their permanent portfolios, accompanied by explanations as to why each was chosen.

High	Medium	Low
• Solution demonstrates that the child knows the concepts and skills. • Solution is complete and thorough. • The child communicates effectively.	• Solution demonstrates that the child has some knowledge of the concepts and skills. • Solution is complete. • The child communicates somewhat clearly.	• Solution shows that the child has little or no grasp of the concepts and skills. • Solution is incomplete or contains major errors. • The child does not communicate effectively.

Children and the assessment process

Involving children in the assessment process is central to the development of their abilities to reflect on their own work, to understand the assessment standards to which they are held accountable, and to take ownership for their own learning. Young children may find the reflective process difficult, but with your coaching, they can develop such skills.

Discussion may be needed to help children better understand your standards for performance. Ask children such questions as, "What does it mean to communicate *clearly*?" "What is a *complete* response?" Some children may want to use the high-medium-low rubric to score their responses. Others may prefer to use a simple visual evaluation, such as these characters:

Participation in peer-assessment tasks will also help children to better understand the performance standards. In pairs or small groups, children can review each other's responses and offer feedback. Opportunities to revise work may then be given.

What Additional Materials Are Needed?

Although manipulative materials are not required for solving the problems in *Reasoning and Patterns,* if they are available in the classroom, some children may find them helpful—for example, base ten blocks, coins, hundred boards, and sets of shapes. Colored pencils or crayons should be readily accessible. Some children may find calculators useful for some of the problems.

Management Chart

Name _____

When a problem or task is completed, shade the box with that number.

1	2	3	4	5	6	7	8	9	10
11	12	13	14	15	16	17	18	19	20
21	22	23	24	25	26	27	28	29	30
31	32	33	34	35	36	37	38	39	40
41	42	43	44	45	46	47	48	49	50
51	52	53	54	55	56	57	58	59	60
61	62	63	64	65	66	67	68	69	70
71	72	73	74	75	76	77	78	79	80
81	82	83	84	85	86	87	88	89	90
91	92	93	94	95	96	97	98	99	100

Award Certificate

Hot Math Topics

SUPER SOLVER

this certifies that

_____

has been awarded the Hot Math Topics Super Solver Certificate for

Excellence in Problem Solving

_____   _____
date   signature

Problems
and Tasks

Use the facts.

Write the name under each boy.

Facts

- Jay is first in line.
- Hani is between Kai and John.
- John is not last.

- -

Where did Nathan's rings land?

- Three of his rings made points.
- Two rings scored the same number of points.
- No ring scored 7.
- Nathan's total score was less than 20.

Masako had 50¢.

She bought 2 items at the yard sale.

Now she has 22¢.

What did she buy?

I have a brother and a sister.

- We are all different ages.
- I am the oldest.
- My sister is the youngest.
- I am 7 years old.
- When you add our 3 ages, you get 17.

How old is my sister?

5

The pattern below continues.

What is letter 45?

Tell how you know.

BOOKBOOKBOOK . . .
1 2 3 4 . . .

- -

Count by 6s.

Color each number you say red.

6

Pick your favorite number
from 1 to 5.

Count by that number.

Color each number you
say blue.

What numbers have
both colors?

What is special about
those numbers?

1	2	3	4	5	6	7	8	9	10
11	12	13	14	15	16	17	18	19	20
21	22	23	24	25	26	27	28	29	30
31	32	33	34	35	36	37	38	39	40
41	42	43	44	45	46	47	48	49	50
51	52	53	54	55	56	57	58	59	60
61	62	63	64	65	66	67	68	69	70
71	72	73	74	75	76	77	78	79	80
81	82	83	84	85	86	87	88	89	90
91	92	93	94	95	96	97	98	99	100

The same letters are the same numbers.

$$
\begin{array}{r}
\text{CD} \\
+ \text{CC} \\
\hline
49
\end{array}
$$

C = __   D = __

- -

8

Count by fives to 50.

How many numbers did you say?

Now, think but don't count.

How many numbers will you say when you count by fives to 100?

Why do you think so?

Look at pattern A and pattern B.

How are the two patterns alike?

How are they different?

Pattern A

Pattern B

You are thinking of the secret number 36.

You make up these 2 clues.

Clues

- My number is between 30 and 40.

- You say it when you count by fours.

-

Make up a third clue.

Give the 3 clues to a friend.

Have your friend tell the secret number.

Choose a number for ☐.

Find △ and ○.

☐ = _____

△ = _____

○ = _____

Choose another number for ☐.

Find △ and ○.

Do this 2 more times. What do you notice?

Do you think this will always happen? Why?

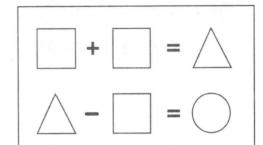

- -

What coins could I have?

Make a list.

- I have 3 coins.
- I have less than 40¢.
- I have more than 20¢.

The ladder pattern continues.

One ladder has 31 ☐.

What is the ladder number?

Tell how you know.

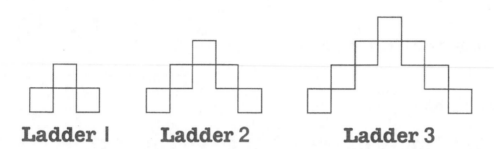

Ladder 1   Ladder 2   Ladder 3

- -

What is the bird's number?

Clues

My number is between 10 and 20.

One of the digits is 1 more than the other digit.

Think of a number.

Make up clues about your number.

Give your clues to a friend.

Make up a rule.

Use your rule to put the numbers into 2 groups.

3   6   36   25
15   40   10   21

How are the numbers in each group alike?

Subtract.

Look for patterns.

Find the ⬡.

```
 100       200       300       400                 
-  3      -  3      -  3      -  3      . . .      -  3
----      ----      ----      ----                ----
  97       197       297       397                 797
```

Use the numbers on the sign.

The story must make sense.

I bought a bike for $_____ .

I bought a water bottle for $_____ .

Altogether I spent $_____ .

I gave the clerk $100.

He gave me $_____ in change.

1	2	3	4	5	6	7	8	9	10
11	12	13	14	15	16	17	18	19	20
21	22	23	24	25	26	27	28	29	30
31	32	33	34	35	36	37	38	39	40

What number is 7 rows below 29?

What number is 6 spaces to the right of 92?

What is the last number in the 10th row?

Finish the sentences.

All of these numbers are _____ .

Some of these numbers are _____ .

None of these numbers is _____ .

Compare your answers with a friend's answers.

Ben, Cari, David, and Eli went bowling.

- Ben did not get the highest score.
- Cari got 19 more points than David.

Write the names on the score card.

Score Card

Name	Score
	118
	81
	94
	100

In pinwheel 20, how many

☐ are there? ____

○ are there? ____

△ are there? ____

Pinwheel I

Pinwheel 2

Pinwheel 3

- -

Row I	1	2	3	4	5
Row 2	6	7	8	9	10
Row 3	11	12	13	14	15
Row 4	16	17	18	19	20
Row 5	21	22	23	24	25
Row 6	26				

The pattern continues.

I00 is the last number in which row?

How do you know?

You toss 2 rings that land on different pegs.

How many different scores are possible?

Make a list.

- -

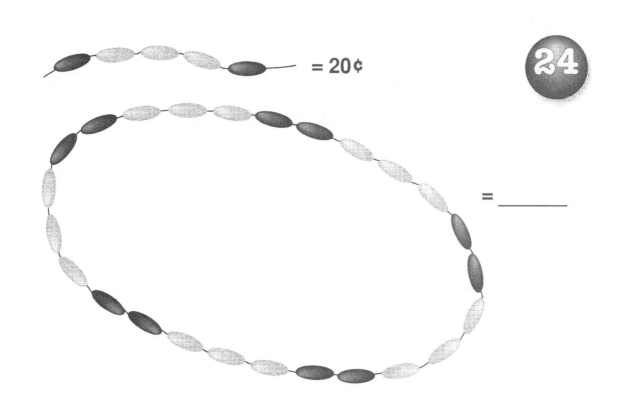

= 20¢

= _____

Use the numbers on the sign.

The story must make sense.

Sara is _____ years old.

She is in grade _____ .

Her brother is _____ years old.

He is _____ years older than Sara.

Their ages add to _____ years.

Fill in the squares.

Add across. Add down.

The numbers in the circles are the sums.

2			③
	4	6	⑮
	8		⑱
⑩	⑫	⑭	

How old could each friend be?
Make up ages to fit the facts.

I am older than Tina.

Mara

I am younger than Mara.

Nigel

Nigel is my twin brother.

Theo

I am younger than Theo.

Tina

_____ **years old** _____ **years old** _____ **years old** _____ **years old**

- -

Sy, Joe, and Ed each have a pig, a horse, or a chicken.

Who has which pet?

I can't have a horse. Horses make me sneeze.

I love my animal.

My pig likes to roll in the mud.

Fill in the missing numbers.

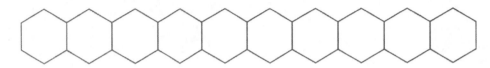

| 53 | | | 44 | 41 | | | 32 | | |

Make your own pattern with missing numbers.

Have a friend fill in the numbers.

Put in +'s and –'s to get the answer.

5 ◯ 4 ◯ 3 ◯ 2 ◯ 1 = 5

Which is more:

- the number of shoes or the number of children in your classroom?

- the number of houses on your street or the number of people who live in them?

- the number of months or the number of days you have lived?

Talk with a friend about how these questions are alike.

Make up two more questions like these.

- -

Make the numbers in the list.

- Use only these numbers:

1 2 4 8

- Use only addition.

For example, 7 = 4 + 2 + 1.

What is the greatest number you can show?

List

$1 = 1$
$2 = 2$
$3 = 1 + 2$
$4 = 4$
$5 = $ _____
$6 = $ _____
$7 = $ _____
$8 = $ _____
$9 = $ _____
.
.
.

33

$$\diagup\!\!\!\!\!\diagdown + 3 = 11$$

$$\diagup\!\!\!\!\!\diagdown + \triangle = 13$$

$$\diagup\!\!\!\!\!\diagdown + \triangle + \hexagon = 15$$

$$\diagup\!\!\!\!\!\diagdown = \underline{\quad}$$

$$\triangle = \underline{\quad}$$

$$\hexagon = \underline{\quad}$$

- -

34

Boxes of Cards Sold

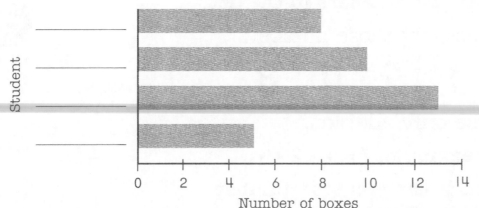

Student

Number of boxes

Bryan, Gia, Paul, and Rosa sold boxes of cards.

How many boxes did each sell?

- Paul sold the least.
- Gia did not sell the most.
- Rosa sold fewer than Gia.

Write the names on the lines.

Add the numbers shown.

Write a number sentence to show the order of the numbers you added.

Add the numbers in a different order.

Write the number sentence.

Compare the sums.

Will this always happen? Why?

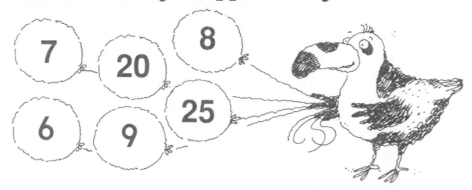

The pattern continues.

Row 1	1	2	3	4
Row 2	5	6	7	8
Row 3	9	10	11	12
Row 4	13	14	15	16
Row 5	17	18	19	20
Row 6	21	22	23	24
Row 7				
Row 8				

What is the first number in row 10?

Make up 3 more questions about the numbers in rows beyond row 6.

Give them to a friend to answer.

Draw picture 10.

Tell how you knew what to draw.

Picture 1	Picture 2	Picture 3	Picture 4	Picture 5

Mia makes bead bracelets just like this.

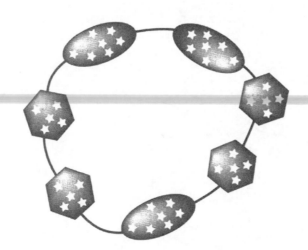

She has 16 and 18 .

How many bracelets can she make?

Tell how you know.

Look at this pattern:

You can show this pattern with letters:

ABBCABBCABBC

Now draw your own shapes to match this pattern:

ABCBABCBABCBABCB

What is U × P?

$$\begin{array}{r} UP \\ + UP \\ \hline 86 \end{array}$$

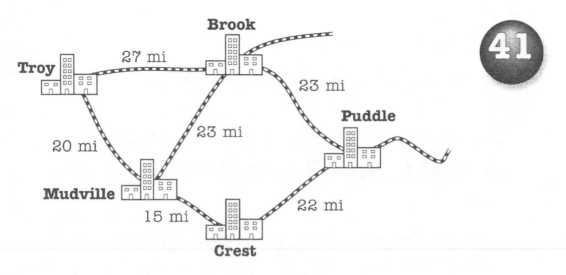

In which city is the swim camp?

- The city's name has fewer than 6 letters.
- The camp is not the same distance from Mudville as it is from Puddle.
- The camp is not 20 miles from Mudville.

- -

 − □ = 10

Put a number in **and a number in**

so the difference is 10.

Add 3 to your number in □ **.**

What must you do to the number in △

so the difference is still 10?

Write each girl's nickname near her.

Our nicknames are Speedy, Sunshine, and Captain.

Karen's nickname is not Sunshine.

Speedy is not Alex's or Karen's nickname.

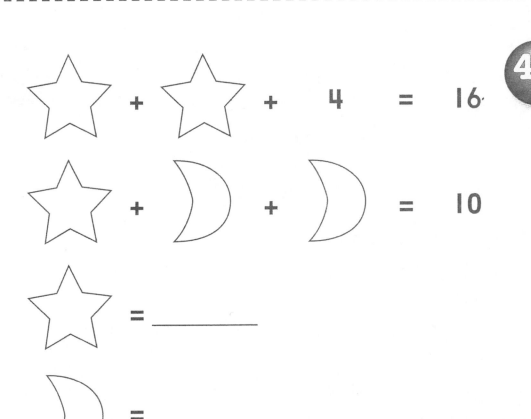

★ + ★ + 4 = 16

★ + ☽ + ☽ = 10

★ = _____

☽ = _____

Use the numbers shown to make addition problems.

45

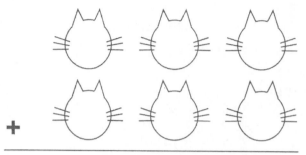

1 2
3 4
5 6

What is the greatest sum you can make?
Write the problem.

What is the least sum you can make?
Write the problem.

How did you decide where to put the numbers?

- -

46

Luis collects stamps.

- He has 4 more stamps from Egypt than from Peru.

- He has 3 fewer stamps from Nigeria than from Egypt.

- He has 27 stamps from Nigeria.

How many stamps does he have from Peru?

5   6   9   15

Which number does not belong?
Why?

Cross it out.

Write a new number in its place.

Is another answer possible?

_____   _____   _____

Rika, Greta, and Bonita each have a favorite color.

- Their favorite colors are red, green, and blue.

- No two girls have the same favorite color.

- No one's favorite color begins with the same letter as her name.

- Rika doesn't like blue.

Write each girl's favorite color.

What's my house number?

- It is between 200 and 300.

- The tens digit is 2 less than the ones digit.

- The ones digit is 7 more than the hundreds digit.

Now write clues for your house or apartment number.

Have a friend find the number.

Wes, Luke, and Tomas live on Oak Street.

Their house colors are white, blue, and green.

Write the house color under each boy.

I don't live in the green house or the white house.

I don't live in the white house.

I don't live in the blue house.

Wes

Luke

Tomas

_____ _____   _____

I am a 2-digit number.

- Reverse my digits and you get a different 2-digit number.

- Add these 2 numbers and you get 66.

What number am I?

Is there another answer?

51

- -

Don't add!

Use A to help you find the answer to B.

52

A	B
43	43
+ 39	+ 29
82	

Tell how you did it.

How many different *dessert specials* are there?

Make a list.

Miki's Dessert Specials

a slice of pie
and a scoop of ice
cream for $3.95

Pies   **Ice Cream**
apple   vanilla
berry   chocolate
pumpkin   mint

How many stamps does Zelika have?

- Zelika has twice as many stamps as Ken.

- Ken has twice as many stamps as Lena.

- Lena has twice as many stamps as Rob.

- Rob has 8 stamps.

How many different 3-digit numbers can you make with the digits 1, 2, 3?

1 2 3

Show the numbers.

Can you make more different 3-digit numbers with the digits 9, 9, 8 than with the digits 1, 2, 3?

9 9 8

Explain.

Carlos bought 10 tickets.

What number is printed on ticket 10?

1	6	11	16	21
Ticket 1	2	3	4	5

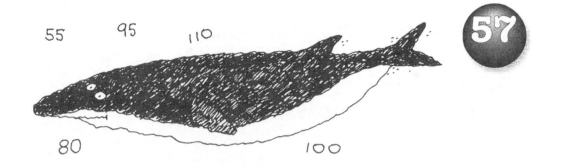

55   95   110

80   100

57

The finback is the second largest whale.

About how many feet long is an adult finback?

Find the length above.

- It is less than 100 feet long.

- It is more than 60 feet long.

- It is not 55 + 40 feet long.

An adult finback is about _____ feet long.

- -

All of these are brimps.

58

None of these are brimps.

Which of these are brimps? How do you know?

A   B   C   D

$$29 + 57 = ?$$

The best estimate for the sum is 70.

The best estimate for the sum is 90.

Do you think Noah or Regina is correct?

Why?

- -

Write the start number.

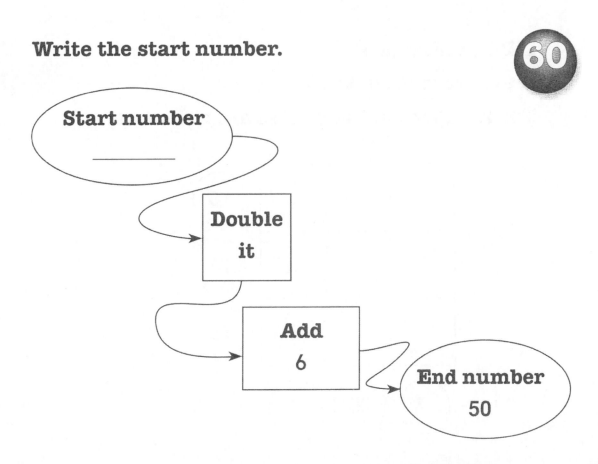

Start number

_____

Double it

Add 6

End number 50

Four numbers are shown above.

Tell how each number is different from the others.

- -

Fill in the squares.

Add across. Add down.

The numbers in the circles are the sums.

			15
5		2	15
	3	6	16
17	20	9	

How much does a weigh?

How much does a weigh?

Tell how you know.

Lani is in the middle of a line of children.

Nat is the 9th child in line.

There are 4 children between Lani and Nat.

How many children are in line?

How many home runs did Babe Ruth hit?

- There is a 4 in the ones place.
- The number is less than 730.
- The number is not equal to 313 + 411.

748   734

724

714   708

The pattern continues.

There are 3 numbers in row 2.

The second number in row 3 is 2.

Row 1				1			
Row 2			2	1	2		
Row 3		3	2	1	2	3	
Row 4	4	3	2	1	2	3	4

How many numbers are in row 100?

What is the fourth number in row 100?

Complete these number sentences.

Fill the ◇.

Use +, −, and ×.

3 ◇ 3 ◇ 3 = 3

3 ◇ 3 ◇ 3 = 6

3 ◇ 3 ◇ 3 = 9

3 ◇ 3 ◇ 3 = 12

3 ◇ 3 ◇ 3 = 27

You take 2 hundreds, 2 tens, and 2 one blocks.

You can use some or all of your blocks.

What numbers can you show with your blocks?

Make a list.

69

You want to round the counting numbers to the nearest 10.

How many numbers will you round to 40?

What are the numbers?

These 4 stickers cost 20¢.

These 4 stickers cost 30¢.

70

How much do these stickers cost?

Tell two ways to find the cost.

42 Hot Math Topics

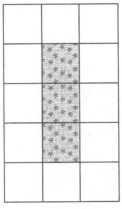

The pattern continues.

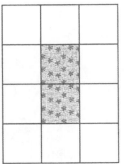

If there are 10 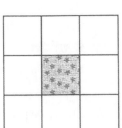, how many are there?

3 fibbles = 4 nibbles

So, 15 fibbles = _____ nibbles

Find a set of 6 numbers that satisfies the clues.

4 of the numbers are even.

4 of the numbers are less than 10.

Compare your set of 6 numbers with a friend's set.

- -

What number comes next?

180   371   562   753   944   ?

Isis, Cal, Sara, Mai, and Sean collected leaves.

- Sara collected 20 fewer leaves than Cal.

- Mai collected the fewest leaves.

- Sean collected more leaves than Isis.

Write the names in the chart.

How many leaves did Sean collect?

Key

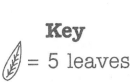 = 5 leaves

Name	Leaves

What numbers between 20 and 35 are **s?**

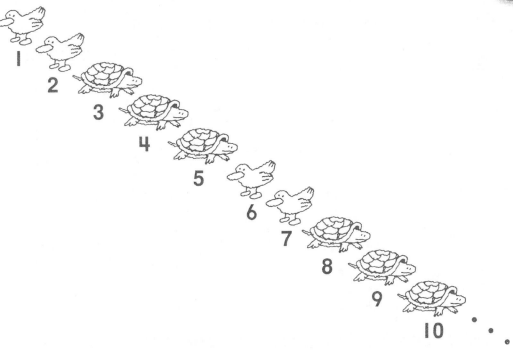

1
2
3
4
5
6
7
8
9
10

Use the numbers on the sign.
The story must make sense.

Building of the Sears Tower began in _____ .

110   1973

1970   1454

The tower was finished
in _____ .

It is the tallest building in
the United States.

It has _____ stories.

It is _____ feet tall.

- -

The pattern continues.
The first number in row 7 is _____ .
The sum of the numbers in row 7 is _____ .

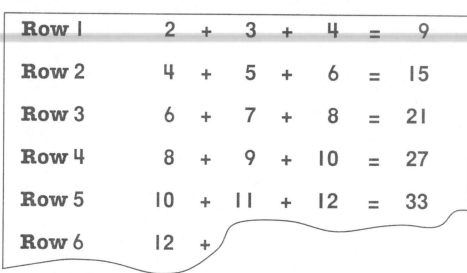

Row 1	2	+	3	+	4	=	9
Row 2	4	+	5	+	6	=	15
Row 3	6	+	7	+	8	=	21
Row 4	8	+	9	+	10	=	27
Row 5	10	+	11	+	12	=	33
Row 6	12	+					

Tell about 2 other patterns you see.

Jamie collects animal cards.

He tacks them on a cork board like this:

 1 card
4 tacks

 2 cards
6 tacks

3 cards
8 tacks

How many tacks will he need for 8 cards?

Tell how you know.

3 stickers for 11¢

You have $1.

You buy star stickers and get some change back.

What is the greatest number of stickers you can buy?

What is the change?

Don't subtract!

Use X to help you find the answer to Y.

X	Y
72	62
−45	−45
27	

Tell how you did it.

- -

Use the numbers from 0 to 8.

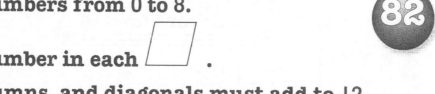

Put one number in each ▱ .

Rows, columns, and diagonals must add to 12.

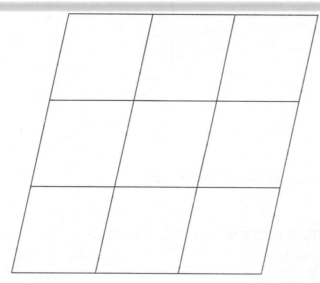

Building 1　　**Building 2**　　**Building 3**　　**83**

1 pentagon
5 toothpicks

2 pentagons
9 toothpicks

3 pentagons
13 toothpicks

• • •

You want to make building 6.

How many toothpicks will you need?

Kurt lined up his cars and trucks in a pattern.　　**84**

- Each car has 4 wheels.

- Each truck has 6 wheels.

He counted 50 wheels.

How many cars are in the line?

Tell how you know.

Put in +'s and –'s to get the answer.

$$9 \bigcirc 7 \bigcirc 5 \bigcirc 3 \bigcirc 1 = 3$$

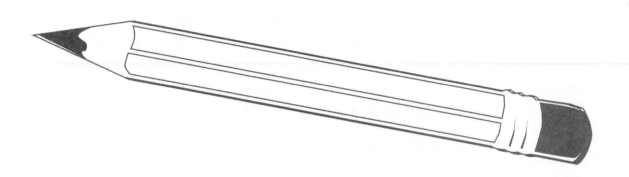

- -

Think of the numbers from 1 to 99.

Are there more even numbers or more odd numbers?

How did you decide?

The pattern below continues for 60 letters.

MOVIESMOVIESMOVIESMOVIESMOVIES . . .

How many letters are vowels?

Tell two ways to decide.

You have 4 , 4 ■, 4 ○, and 4 ||| tiles.

Draw your 16 tiles in the grid.

• Every row must have 1 of each kind.

• Every column must have 1 of each kind.

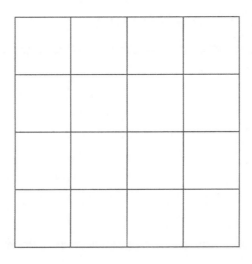

**How many people are in line for
the roller coaster?**

- There are more than 125 people.
- There are fewer than 600 people.
- There is an even number of people.
- The hundreds digit is less than
  the ones digit.
- There are not 376 people.

690   468   376

100   257   582

Pedro drew a picture worth 36 points.

He drew triangles and squares.

He drew more than 3 squares.

Make a picture Pedro could have drawn.

Pedro's Picture

4 points

3 points

The heart is doing something special to these numbers.

Tell what the heart is doing.

2 ♡ 1 = 4   5 ♡ 1 = 7

4 ♡ 0 = 4   6 ♡ 0 = 6

5 ♡ 3 = 11   10 ♡ 3 = 16

0 ♡ 4 = 8   0 ♡ 10 = 20

Solve these heart problems.

3 ♡ 0 = _____   8 ♡ 3 = _____

6 ♡ 1 = _____   0 ♡ 9 = _____

- -

Ms. Shaw's class is planning a cookie sale.

They want to decide what types of cookies to sell.

They are asking their friends questions to help them decide.

Whose question do you think is better, Lana's or Maria's? Why?

1 8   4   5   3   6

93

Use the numbers above.

Fill in the empty squares and circles.

The numbers in the circles are the sums.

- Row 1 has only even numbers.
- Row 3 has only odd numbers.
- The numbers in row 2 are in counting order.

Row 1				18
Row 2		2		◯
Row 3	7		9	◯

◯ 12   ◯   ◯ 18

94

Gia and José are playing _Trade It._

In the game, 4 are worth 2 .

At the end of the game,

Gia has 12  **and José has 5** .

Whose cards are worth more?

Tell how you know.

Use the numbers on the sign.

The story must make sense.

Abraham Lincoln was born in February of the year _____ .

He was elected president of the U.S. in the year _____ .

He was the _____th president.

He was president for about _____ years.

He died at the age of _____ years.

- -

There are 2 red squares in the Shape Set.

Write a number on each line.

Red   Square

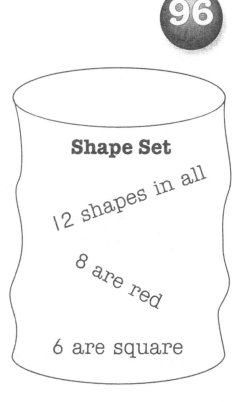

Shape Set

12 shapes in all

8 are red

6 are square

How many shapes are red and not square?

How many shapes are square and not red?

This bead chain has a pattern.

Some of the beads are in the box.

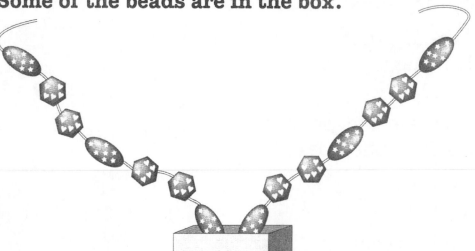

How many  could be in the bead chain?

Tell how you know.

- -

The ![cylinder] weighs the same as ![two balls] .

What do you know about the weight of the  ?

The number pattern continues.

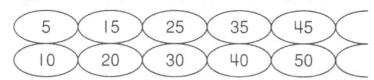

Follow the arrows.

$15 \leftarrow = 5$ $30 \rightarrow = 40$ $70 \leftarrow \leftarrow = 50$ $45 \rightarrow \rightarrow = 65$

Fill in the missing numbers.

$80 \rightarrow = \underline{\hspace{1cm}}$ $75 \rightarrow \rightarrow = \underline{\hspace{1cm}}$ $25 \leftarrow \rightarrow = \underline{\hspace{1cm}}$

$65 \rightarrow \rightarrow = \underline{\hspace{1cm}}$ $90 \rightarrow \rightarrow \leftarrow = \underline{\hspace{1cm}}$ $120 \leftarrow \leftarrow \rightarrow = \underline{\hspace{1cm}}$

- -

The pattern continues.

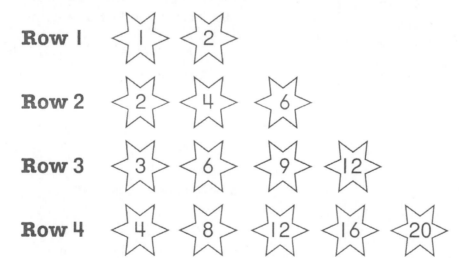

Row 1

Row 2

Row 3

Row 4

What is the last number in row 10?

Tell how you know.

Answers

1. from first in line to last: Jay, John, Hani, Kai

2. two on 4 and one on 10

3. puzzle and toy truck

4. 4 years old

5. B; Explanations will vary.

6. Answers will vary. Numbers colored red are multiples of 6. Numbers colored blue are multiplies of the favorite number. Multiples of both numbers have both colors.

7. 2, 7

8. 10, 20; Explanations will vary.

9. Answers will vary.

10. Possible clue: You say it when you count by threes.

11. Numbers will vary. The triangle is twice the square, and the circle and the square are equal. Possible explanation: Adding a number to itself gives twice that number, and subtracting a number from twice a number gives that number.

12.

P	N	D	Q
2			1
1	1		1
	2		1
1		1	1
1		2	
	1	2	
		3	

13. 15; Explanations will vary.

14. 12; Clues will vary.

15. 89, 4, 93, 7

16. 99, 98, 100

17. Answers will vary.

18. 800

19. Possible answer: odd numbers, 2-digit numbers, even

20. from top to bottom: Eli, David, Ben, Cari

21. 1, 80, 4

22. row 20; Possible explanation: The last number is 5 times the row number.

23. 6 scores: 17, 22, 25, 32, 35, 40

24. 100¢ or $1

25. 7, 2, 16, 9, 23

26.

2	0	1
5	4	6
3	8	7

27. Ages will vary. Mara is the oldest, Tina is the youngest, and Theo and Nigel are the same age.

28. Joe, chicken; Sy, horse; Ed, pig

29. 53 50 47 44 41 38 35 32 29 26
Patterns will vary.

30. Possible answers: 5 + 4 − 3 − 2 + 1 = 5 or 5 − 4 + 3 + 2 − 1 = 5

31. shoes, people, days; Answers and questions will vary.

32. The greatest number is 15.

    5 = 4 + 1   11 = 8 + 2 + 1
    6 = 4 + 2   12 = 8 + 4
    7 = 4 + 2 + 1   13 = 8 + 4 + 1
    8 = 8   14 = 8 + 4 + 2
    9 = 8 + 1   15 = 8 + 4 + 2 + 1
    10 = 8 + 2

33. 8, 5, 2

34. from top to bottom: Rosa, Gia, Bryan, Paul

35. 75; The sums are the same. Changing the order doesn't change the sum.

36. 37; Questions will vary.

37. Explanations will vary. Possible arrangements:

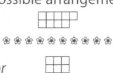

or

38. 4 bracelets; Possible explanation: She uses 16 🛑 and 12 🛑 for 4 bracelets. For 5 bracelets, she would need 20 🛑, which she doesn't have.

39. Shapes will vary.

40. 12

41. Crest

42. Increase it by 3.

43. Beth, Speedy; Alex, Sunshine; Karen, Captain

44. 6, 2

45. 1173, 381; Problems and explanations will vary.

46. 26 stamps

47. Answers will vary.

48. Rika, green; Greta, blue; Bonita, red

49. 279; Clues will vary.

50. Wes, blue; Luke, green; Tomas, white

51. 15, 51, 24, or 42

52. 72; Since 29 is 10 less than 39, the sum of B will be 10 less than the sum of A.

53. 9 specials: apple, vanilla; apple, chocolate; apple, mint; berry, vanilla; berry, chocolate; berry, mint; pumpkin, vanilla; pumpkin, chocolate; pumpkin, mint

54. 64 stamps

55. With 1, 2, 3 you can make 6 numbers: 123, 132, 213, 231, 321,

312. With 9, 9, 8 you can make only 3 numbers: 899, 989, 998.

56. 46

57. 80

58. C and D; Brimps have 4 sides, with a black triangle in one corner and an open circle with 2 line segments in another corner.

59. Answers will vary. For a quick answer, adding the tens (as Noah has done) might be fine. For a closer estimate, rounding first (as Regina has done) is better.

60. 22

61. Possible answer: 2 is the only single-digit number, 106 is the only 3-digit number, 66 is the only number with a repeated digit, and 15 is the only odd number.

62.

5	9	1
5	8	2
7	3	6

63. 3 kg, 2 kg; Explanations will vary.

64. 27 children

65. 714

66. 199, 97

67. $3 + 3 - 3 = 3$ or $3 - 3 + 3 = 3$
$3 \times 3 - 3 = 6$
$3 + 3 + 3 = 9$
$3 \times 3 + 3 = 12$ or $3 + 3 \times 3 = 12$
$3 \times 3 \times 3 = 27$

68. 1, 2, 10, 11, 12, 20, 21, 22, 100, 101, 102, 110, 111, 112, 120, 121, 122, 200, 201, 202, 210, 211, 212, 220, 221, 222

69. 10 numbers: 35, 36, 37, 38, 39, 40, 41, 42, 43, 44

70. 40¢; Possible explanations: 4 apples are 20¢ so 1 apple is 5¢; 5¢ + banana + 5¢ + banana = 30¢, so 2 bananas = 20¢, so 1 banana = 10¢;

4 apples + 2 bananas = 20¢ + 20¢ = 40¢.
Or, 2 apples are 10¢, and
10¢ + 2 bananas = 30¢, so
2 bananas = 20¢ and 1 banana = 10¢;
4 apples + 2 bananas = 20¢ + 20¢ = 40¢.

71. 26

72. 20

73. Answers will vary.

74. 1135

75. from top to bottom: Mai, Sara, Sean, Isis, Cal; 40 leaves

76. 21, 22, 26, 27, 31, 32

77. 1970, 1973, 110, 1454

78. 14, 45; Patterns will vary.

79. 18 tacks; Explanations will vary.

80. 27 stickers, 1¢

81. 17; Since 72 is 10 more than 62, the answer to X is 10 more than the answer to Y.

82. Possible grid:

3	2	7
8	4	0
1	6	5

83. 25 toothpicks

84. 5 cars; Explanations will vary.

85. 9 − 7 + 5 − 3 − 1 = 3

86. There are more odd numbers (50 odd and 49 even). Explanations will vary.

87. 30 letters; Possible explanations: "MOVIES" will repeat 10 times, and there are 3 vowels each time. *Or,* half of the letters are vowels, and half of 60 is 30.

88. Possible grid:

89. 468 people

90. Pictures should have 6 squares and 4 triangles.

91. The heart adds the first number to twice the second number; from left to right: 3, 14, 8, 18.

92. Answers will vary. Which question is better depends on the situation. If they can make only chocolate chip or peanut butter cookies, Lana's question is better. If they want to identify the favorite type to be able to make the most of those, Maria's question is better.

93.

Row 1	4	8	6	⑱
Row 2	1	2	3	⑥
Row 3	7	5	9	㉑
	⑫	⑮	⑱	

94. Gia's; Possible explanation: 4 ponds = 2 snowmen, so 12 ponds = 6 snowmen. José's 5 snowmen are worth less than Gia's 12 ponds.

95. 1809, 1860, 16, $4\frac{1}{4}$, 56

96. 6, 2, 4 (in the circles); 6; 4

97. 10 or 12 or 14 . . .; Explanations will vary.

98. Possible answer: The weighs less than the ●. The weighs half as much as the ● and one fourth as much as the . The ● weighs twice as much as the .

99. from left to right: 90, 95, 25, 85, 100, 110

100. 110; Numbers in row 10 increase by 10s, and there will be 11 numbers in that row.